ALEX RODRIGUEZ

DISCOVER THE LIFE OF A SPORTS STAR

David and Patricia Armentrout

Rourke

Publishing LLC

Vero Beach, Florida 32964

www.rourkepublishing.com

PHOTO CREDITS: All photos © Getty Images

Title page: *A-Rod led the American League in home runs during the 2002 season.*

Editor: Frank Sloan

Cover and interior design by Nicola Stratford

Library of Congress Cataloging-in-Publication Data

Armentrout, David, 1962-
  Alex Rodriguez / David Armentrout and Patricia Armentrout.
     v. cm. — (Discover the life of a sports star)
Includes bibliographical references and index.
Contents: A dream come true — Alex Rodriguez — Land of baseball -- A
new home — A role model — Number one draft pick — First Major League
game — A-Rod — Texas Rangers.
  ISBN 1-58952-654-6 (hardcover)
  1. Rodriguez, Alex, 1975—Juvenile literature. 2. Baseball
players—United States—Biography—Juvenile literature. [1. Rodriguez,
Alex, 1975- 2. Baseball players. 3. Dominican Americans--Biography.] I.
Armentrout, Patricia, 1960- II. Title. III. Series: Armentrout,
David, 1962- Discover the life of a sports star.
  GV865.R62A76 2003
  796.357'092—dc21

Printed in the USA

CG/CG

Table of Contents

The Texas Rangers have seen their game attendance increase since signing Alex.

A Dream Come True

As a boy, Alex Rodriguez dreamed of being a **professional** baseball player. Not everyone who dreams of being a professional ball player makes it. However, Alex Rodriguez's dream came true. He is one of the best players in professional baseball.

Nickname:
A-Rod
Team:
Texas Rangers
Position: Shortstop, bats right, throws right
Number: 3
Record: Led the American League in home runs in 2002

Alex Rodriguez

Alex's parents are from the Dominican Republic, a poor island country in the **Caribbean**. Before Alex was born, his family moved to New York City looking for a better life.

Alex was born to Victor and Lourdes Rodriguez in New York City in 1975. Victor eventually grew tired of the hectic life in New York and moved his family back to the Dominican Republic.

Alex lived in the Dominican Republic for several years during his childhood, but has lived most of his life in the United States.

Slugger Sammy Sosa is one of many great baseball players from the Dominican Republic.

Land of Baseball

Baseball is the most popular sport in the Dominican Republic. It was there that Alex learned to love the game. The weather in the Caribbean is always warm. Children and adults can play baseball almost every day of the year. Many great ball players have come from this island nation. They know that if they make it to the **major leagues** in the United States, they will earn a great living playing their favorite game.

Alex has played baseball since he was a young boy.

A New Home

Alex and his family moved back to the United States when Alex was eight years old. This time, they settled in a town near Miami, Florida. Alex went to school and played baseball. Everything was going well.

When Alex turned nine, his life changed forever. His father left the family and moved to New York City. Victor would never again play a big role in Alex's life.

Alex was thrilled to be able to play against his boyhood idol Cal Ripkin, Jr.

A Role Model

Alex continued to play baseball. When he had time, Alex watched major league players on television. He studied the way they played. He also paid attention to the way they handled themselves on and off the field. One of Alex's baseball heroes was Cal Ripken, Jr. Ripken is known for his skill as a shortstop and also for his winning attitude on and off the field.

Number One Draft Pick

In high school, Alex excelled at football and basketball. In the end, however, he decided to focus on baseball. In 1992, his high school baseball team was ranked the best high school team in the country. Alex's last year in high school was in 1993. He would have to make a career decision. He could play for a college team, or he could go directly to the pros. The Seattle Mariners helped Alex make his decision. In the **draft pick** of 1993, they chose Alex as number one.

The Seattle Mariners made Alex the top draft pick of 1993 and signed him to a $13 million contract.

First Major League Game

After less than a year playing **minor league** ball for the Seattle Mariners, Alex was promoted to the major leagues. He played his first major league game against the Boston Red Sox. During the next couple of years, Alex was sent back and forth between the major and minor leagues. Alex became close friends with Ken Griffey, Jr., a star player with the Mariners. Griffey helped Alex adjust to the highs and lows of professional baseball.

Ken Griffey, Jr. and A-Rod exchange high-fives during a game against the San Diego Padres.

The 2000 season was Alex's last as a Seattle Mariner.

A-Rod

   Alex, or "A-Rod," as his fans call him, began the 1996 season as the starting shortstop for the Mariners. The 1996 season was spectacular for Alex. He led the American League in hits and runs scored. The Mariners were impressed. They offered Alex a 4-year $10 million contract.

   Alex helped the Mariners become one of the best teams in baseball during the 2000 season. The Mariners made it all the way to the American League **pennant** series.

Texas Rangers

Alex became a **free agent** at the end of the 2000 season. Many major league teams offered Alex contracts. After weeks of talks, an amazing deal was made with the Texas Rangers. Alex signed a 10-year, $252 million contract. Texas Ranger fans have not been disappointed.

In the 2002 season, Alex led the American League in home runs and runs batted in. In the years to come, Alex will continue to entertain baseball fans with his achievements on and off the field.

In 2000 A-Rod signed the largest baseball contract in history with the Texas Rangers.

Dates to Remember

1975	Born in New York
1992	High school baseball team ranked number one in the country
1993	Number one draft pick
1996	Leads the league in batting average and runs scored
1998	Third major league player to hit 40 home runs and steal 40 bases in the same year
2000	Selected Major League Player of the Year by Baseball America
2000	Signs $252 million contract with Texas Rangers
2002	Leads the American League in home runs and runs batted in

Glossary

Caribbean (kah RIB ee uhn) — the sea near the Atlantic Ocean between North and South America

draft pick (DRAFT pik) — a player selected by a team through a procedure agreed upon by a league

free agent (FREE AY juhnt) — not bound to a contract; free to sign with any team

major leagues (MAY jur LEEGZ) — the highest level of professional baseball

minor league (MY nur LEEG) — professional baseball at a level below the majors

pennant (PEN uhnt) — league championship

professional (pruh FESH un ul) — a good athlete who is paid for his or her skill

Index

Further Reading

Gallagher, Jim. *Alex Rodriguez: Latinos in Baseball*.
   Mitchell Lane Publishers, Inc., 2000.
MacNow, Glen. *Sports Great: Alex Rodriguez*. Enslow Publishers, Inc., 2002.
Stout, Glen. *On the Field with Alex Rodriguez*. Little, Brown & Co 2002.

Websites To Visit

sports.espn.go.com/mlb/players/profile?statsId=5275
bigleaguers.yahoo.com/mlb/players/5/5275/
mlb.com

About The Authors

David and Patricia Armentrout have written many nonfiction books for young readers.
They have had several books published for primary school reading. The Armentrouts
live in Cincinnati, Ohio, with their two children.